Creepy Chicago

A Ghosthunter's Tales of the City's Scariest Sites

By Ursula Bielski

Illustrated by Amy Noble

First Edition

www.lakeclaremont.com
Chicago

Creepy Chicago: A Ghosthunter's Tales of the City's Scariest Sites
by Ursula Bielski

Published August, 2003 by:

 www.lakeclaremont.com

Copyright © 2003 by Ursula Bielski

Publisher's Cataloging-in-Publication
(Provided by Quality Books, Inc.)

Bielski, Ursula.
   Creepy Chicago : a ghosthunter's tales of the city's
scariest sites / by Ursula Bielski ; illustrated by Amy
Noble. — 1st ed.
   p. cm.
   Includes index.
   Audience: Ages 8-12.
   LCCN 2003105153
   ISBN 1-893121-15-1

   1. Haunted places—Illinois—Chicago—Juvenile
literature. 2. Ghosts—Illinois—Chicago—Juvenile
literature. [1. Ghosts—Illinois—Chicago.]   I. Noble,
Amy. II. Title.

BF1472.U6B54 2003   133.1'09773'11
                    QBI33-1437

**Printed in the United States of America by United Graphics,
an employee-owned company based in Mattoon, Illinois.**

08 07 06   10 9 8 7 6 5 4 3

For Eva and Ilse

Publisher Credits
Cover design by Timothy Kocher. Illustrations by Amy Noble.
Illustration help by Joe Somers of Squibbles Ink, Inc. Interior
design and layout by Sharon Woodhouse. Editing by Patricia
Kummer. Proofreading by Ken Woodhouse, Karen Formanski,
and Sharon Woodhouse. Index by Karen Formanski and Ken
Woodhouse. Advanced reading and kid advice from Nikki
Figueroa, Billy Figueroa, Lori Kattner, and Danielle Kattner.

Table of Contents

Preface

You are about to take an armchair excursion through one of America's greatest cities—Chicago!

Like the millions of tourists who visit "The Windy City" each year, you'll make stops at world-famous museums, marvel at towering skyscrapers, explore the town's terrific neighborhoods, and speed along the shore of Lake Michigan on fabulous Lake Shore Drive. But unlike those other tourists, we won't be searching for priceless paintings, pioneering architecture, local heritage or luscious views. We're on the lookout for . . . g-g-g-g-ghosts!

Chicago's history is full of scary stories, terrible fires, hard times, and the toughest gangsters ever known. What's more, Chicagoans have always loved to tell of terrifying events that happened—and still happen—to ordinary people. Hitchhiking phantoms, mysterious handprints, perfectly preserved corpses: tales of these and other oddities are told every day in each of the city's neighborhoods, making Chicago's supernatural folklore some of the strangest in the world. But this folklore tells more than mere ghost stories; it tells a lot about the many kinds of people that have lived—and died—in this endlessly intriguing city.

So turn down the lights and get ready for a very "spirited" journey.

We're off on a whirlwind ride through the world's biggest ghost town!

Creepy Chicago

Skeleton Remains of Fort Dearborn

1

Fort Dearborn:
The Many Haunts of
Chicago's Oldest Ghosts

By most accounts, the haunting of Chicago began in the summer of 1812. At that time, Chicago was not yet named Chicago. It was just a small settlement and military post called Fort Dearborn. Fort Dearborn was home to Chicago's first white settlers.

The fort stood near the mouth of the Chicago River. That is where the river joins Lake Michigan and where the Michigan Avenue bridge is today. In fact, if you travel downtown to the bridge, you can see the outline of the fort in the sidewalk. Pieces of metal in the cement mark where the fort once stood. In the side of the bridge next to these metal markers are sculptures of scenes from Fort Dearborn's history.

When the fort was built in 1803, Native Americans were living in the area. The arrival of white soldiers and settlers greatly disrupted the Native Americans' way of life. Although the two groups didn't always get along, they kept things peaceful for the most part. That is, until a war broke out.

The Fort Dearborn Massacre

In 1812, fighting began between the United States and Great Britain. Some groups of Native Americans sided with the British. The settlers and soldiers living at Fort Dearborn were ordered to leave the settlement in case it was attacked. Nearly 150 of them began the long trip east on foot toward Fort Wayne, Indiana. There they could safely live until the fighting ended. However, they never made it.

When the group reached the sand dunes along the shore of Lake Michigan, near what is now 16th Street and Indiana Avenue, a band of Native Americans loyal to the British attacked. The Native Americans killed most of the settlers and took the rest prisoner. This was known as the Fort Dearborn Massacre. Some of the prisoners later died. Others were kept as hostages and sold to the British. After killing the settlers, the Indians returned to Fort Dearborn and burned it to the ground. Some Soldiers who had remained behind burned with the fort.

Fort Dearborn's Ghosts

The bodies of the victims of the Fort Dearborn Massacre were left on the sand dunes, exactly as they had fallen. When American soldiers returned in 1816 to rebuild the fort, they found the victims' skeletons still in the sand, right where they had died. Many years later Chicago was established as a city and the area of the massacre was developed. At that time people started to see strange things near the massacre site, including figures that seemed to float above the ground. These figures were described as looking "old-fashioned." They wore odd clothes from an earlier time and looked lost and sad. These figures continued to be seen until a statue was built on the site ninety years later as a memorial to the massacre victims.

The victims of the Fort Dearborn Massacre seem to have stopped haunting the place where they died. The same is not true of the soldiers who reportedly died in the fire at the fort itself. Sometimes, passersby on the Michigan Avenue bridge are startled to see soldiers marching there. These ghost soldiers are dressed in old-fashioned military clothes. The soldiers quickly disappear after appearing for only a few moments!

Another Old Ghost

Another Fort Dearborn phantom doesn't haunt the fort's former site. Instead, this ghost shows up at a totally different place—a nightclub called Excalibur. This club is located in a popular tourist area about a mile away from the former fort. Many people who have gone to Excalibur to dance report having seen a ghostly figure slipping through the halls and up the stairs. Bartenders at the club have also complained that some invisible person keeps breaking all of the glasses behind the bar!

Some ghosthunters think Excalibur is haunted by a man named John Lalime. Lalime was supposedly killed by Chicago's first white settler, John Kinzie. Kinzie fought with Lalime over the ownership of his cabin. This house was located directly across the river from Fort Dearborn. After Kinzie killed Lalime, he buried him in the front yard of the cabin. Lalime's bones didn't stay there though. They were later dug up and given to the Chicago Historical Society. At one time the Chicago Historical Society was located on the same site the Excalibur nightclub occupies today.

Some people familiar with the story believe that Lalime wants his bones returned to the grave on the property he claimed was his. Too bad—he'll never get his wish. The old Historical Society building burned to the ground during the Great Chicago Fire of 1871. Everything inside was destroyed, including priceless documents, precious artifacts . . . and the bones of John Lalime.

2

The Graveyards of Archer Avenue: On the Road with Some Famous Phantoms

Judging by appearance alone, it's no surprise that Archer Avenue is known as one of the most haunted stretches of roadway in the world. There's more to this area's reputation than looks alone, however. Just ask the people who live in the suburbs southwest of Chicago, through which Archer Avenue runs. These residents have long believed that countless phantoms really do live

The Famous Resurrection Mary

in the many cemeteries and forest preserves along this creepy section of highway.

Archer Avenue was once an old Indian trail. In the early 1800s, it was made into a road by Irish immigrants. They had come to Chicago to build the nearby Illinois and Michigan Canal. One of Archer's most haunted sites is an old churchyard in which many of these workers are buried.

St. James-Sag Cemetery

For more than one hundred years, St. James, Sag Bridge, has been the site of numerous "hauntings." They began in the late 1800s. During those years, witnesses first reported seeing phantom, hooded monks floating over the graveyard's hilly landscape. Other ghosts said to reside there include those of a young man and woman who had once worked at the parish rectory in the late 1800s. While trying to run away and get married one summer's night, they were killed instead when their horse and carriage crashed. Legend says that their ghostly carriage still bolts through the trees off Archer Avenue just beyond the church's front gate.

At times, strange voices and chants can also be heard inside the cemetery and the forest preserve surrounding it. Occasionally, people in the area late at night report having seen hooded, floating figures. They are the same figures that were first observed there passing silently over the graveyard's back ridge more than a century ago.

Maple Lake

Not far from St. James is Maple Lake, another popular site for local ghosthunters eager to spot some eerie presence. On clear nights, it's not uncommon to see cars parked along the 95th Street Overlook. Their passengers scan the water for a glimpse of the lake's world-famous "ghost light." This light is a mysterious glowing ball that bobs among the trees before winking out like a light bulb.

Archer Woods Cemetery

A little further up Archer at Kean Road is another graveyard, Archer Woods. This cemetery is home to "The Wailing Woman." She is a wandering spirit who walks sadly through the trees of this isolated site. She sobs and cries out to passersby. While all of these hauntings have combined to establish Archer Avenue's paranormal reputation, the road's mosthaunted stretch lies just north of Archer Woods Cemetery. There, alongside Resurrection Cemetery, lurks Chicago's most famous phantom: "Resurrection Mary."

Resurrection Cemetery and "Resurrection Mary"

For many years, ghosts like "Resurrection

Mary" have been reported in all corners of the world. Known as "phantom hitchhikers," they have been seen in nightclubs and along dark roads. They usually appear to young men who are attracted to their great beauty.

The woman known as "Resurrection Mary" was first seen by visitors to popular ballrooms on the Chicago's South Side in the 1930s. After spotting the beautiful girl with long blonde hair dressed all in white, a man would dance with her the entire night. Yet, she rarely spoke or even looked her dance partner in the eye. At the end of the evening, the mysterious girl would suddenly become worried. She would beg frantically for a ride home. Thrilled at the chance to escort such a beauty, the young man with whom Mary had danced was always quick to oblige.

Once in the car, Mary would give her potential suitor vague directions. She would say only that she lived "up Archer." Then, as the car neared the main gates of Resurrection Cemetery, instead of a kiss goodnight, the driver would get the scare of his life. That's when Mary would suddenly open the passenger door and jump out of the car. She would run *through* the cemetery's locked gates and disappear into the blackness of the graveyard beyond!

Over the years, incidents like that have occurred repeatedly to dozens of unsuspecting young men. Most accounts are nearly identical. However, a few differ slightly. Instead of picking Mary up at a dance, some men claim to have run over her in the road! After hitting a woman, who seemingly appears from out of thin air, these startled drivers pull over to help their victim. Mary, however, is nowhere to be found.

On one occasion, Mary left some permanent evidence of her existence. Around midnight one night in the 1970s, a motorist was driving past the front entrance of Resurrection Cemetery. He saw a young woman staring out from the locked iron gates. Her hands were clutching the bars in fear. Figuring that the woman had accidentally been locked inside the cemetery after closing time, the man called police. He told them to go to the cemetery and let her out.

When police arrived, they found no one! Then something else made their blood run cold. The steel bars of the cemetery gate had been pried apart at the exact spot where the young woman had been seen. Branded into the metal—as if by an incredible heat—was the impression of two small handprints!

For weeks after, people came from all around to view the bars that bore what they believed were the handprints of Resurrection Mary. After a while, the crowds became bothersome. To discourage people from coming to see the handprints, the cemetery officials finally had the bars taken down and repaired.

Even today visitors can still see the spot where Mary's handprints once appeared. Despite having been painted over, the metal remains eerily discolored and resistant to cleaning.

Why Is Archer Avenue Haunted?

No one knows for sure why Archer Avenue is as haunted as it apparently is. Some think the answer lies in its origin as a Native American trail. Perhaps Native Americans built the road over a sacred path that they knew to be filled with spiritual energy. Other experts on the paranormal believe that waterways are conductors of such energy. These experts point to large number of rivers, canals, and streams in the area to explain why strange sightings are so plentiful there. Still others credit the suffering and death of the Irish canal workers for the strange sightings along this stretch of road. They believe that the workers' ghosts cursed the road because they built the road under such miserable working conditions.

Whatever the case, one thing remains certain: The rich folklore and naturally "haunting" atmosphere of this area will keep travelers to Archer Avenue spooked for generations to come.

Robinson Woods: An Enchanted Forest?

3

Robinson Woods:
An Enchanted Forest
on the Northwest Side

As you walk through Che-che-pin-quay Woods, you may be surprised to find yourself in a graveyard! This woods is also known as Robinson Woods. It is in the forest preserves along River Road on Chicago's far Northwest Side.

Before this land was a public forest preserve, it was the home—and burial site—of

Alexander Robinson's family. He was a very important person in the early days of Chicago's history.

Who Was Alexander Robinson?

Alexander Robinson came from a mixed-blood family. That means that one parent was Anglo or white, and one parent was Native American. As a young man, Robinson married Catherine Chevalier, the daughter of a Potawatomi chief. After his father-in-law died, Alexander Robinson became the tribe's new chief. That's when he was given the new Native American name of "Che-che-pin-quay." This means "winking eye."

Robinson was a peace-loving person. He wanted to use his understanding of both Native American and white cultures to help the two groups live peacefully together. Robinson spent many years working as an interpreter. He helped Chicago's Native Americans and white settlers understand and get along with one another. In fact,

Robinson did so much to help keep the peace during Chicago's difficult early years that the city government gave him a gift in 1829: a big piece of land along the Des Plaines River, in the exact spot that Robinson Woods now stands.

Many years passed before Alexander Robinson and his family actually settled on that land. He still had a lot of work to do. When Robinson finally did move there, he enjoyed many peaceful years until he died in 1872. After his death, Robinson's family continued to live on the land until their house burned down.

Strange Happenings in Robinson Woods

The Robinson family graves in Robinson Woods were said to have been peaceful, too. Then something happened to upset the spirits of the family. In 1973, the last of Alexander Robinson's descendants died. The City of Chicago wouldn't allow this person's body to be buried in the family cemetery in Robinson Woods. That's when all sorts of strange things started to happen at the burial ground. Hikers reported seeing weird lights and faces peeking out from between the trees. They also heard the drumbeat of tom-toms coming from nowhere. Near the boulder that marks the Robinson family graves, people have smelled the strong scent of lilac bushes in the dead of winter.

While visiting these woods, many psychics have seen unusual visions. Some of these psychics claim that they received messages from figures that they describe as being Native American. Other parapsychologists—people who study ghosts—also get the creeps there. They are convinced that something strange is indeed happening at Robinson Woods. One group of investigators was able to record the mysterious drumbeats on audiotape. Many others have taken photographs of the strange faces seen between the trees.

So, the next time you decide to take a hike and want to see something unusual, head to Robinson Woods. Don't forget your camera and your tape recorder. You might collect some interesting evidence. Be sure to bring along a sweatshirt. You're sure to get the chills in this truly enchanted forest.

Weirdness in Streeterville

4

Streeterville:
Weirdness—and Weirdos—in the
Fanciest Neighborhood in Town

What do mysterious deaths, freak accidents, a colony of marching spiders, devil worshipers, and a mad sailor have in common? They're all part of the weird history of Chicago's super-ritzy Streeterville neighborhood!

This fashionable lakefront area has long been known for its pricey shops, fine hotels, and lovely, flower-lined streets. In fact, one of its streeets—North Michigan Avenue—is called the "Magnificent Mile." Streeterville has also been known even longer as a "not-quite-right" kind of place. A place where the darkly bizarre is always lurking just beneath the glitzy surface.

The Water Tower and "Cap" Streeter's Curse

Historians, folklorists, and ghosthunters each have differing explanations for the neighborhood's reputation. Some say the old Water Tower is the source of the bad vibes that seem to run through the area and its history. The Water Tower is one of the only buildings to survive the Great Chicago Fire of 1871. Over the years, a few passers-by have seen a shadowy figure "hanging" in an upper window of the tower. Beyond this, not much paranormal activity has actually been reported there.

Some others say this section of town was cursed long ago by a crazy seafarer named "Cap" Streeter. Streeter lived on the land that now makes up Streeterville. He claimed that it belonged to him. City officials claimed the land belonged to Chicago. Streeter tried for years to get "rightful" ownership of it, but without much luck. Before Streeter died, he is said to have cursed the land so that the city would be punished for stealing it from him.

The John Hancock Building and the Church of Satan

Still others say a skyscraper is to blame! Since its completion in 1968, the towering John Hancock Building has often been the sight of unexplained deaths and terrible accidents. In addition, a colony of spiders reportedly makes its way up one side of the building and down the other, over and over, year after year.

Strangely enough, many years before the John Hancock building went up, a man named Anton LaVey was born on this site. LaVey grew up to become the founder of the infamous Church of Satan. This religious cult had some rather unusual beliefs. Most people thought LaVey was a crackpot, but he did have some interesting ideas. For example, LaVey believed that certain buildings can have strange effects on the people living in them. If their rooms have strangely angled walls, the people inside can feel strange, too, and also be led to do strange things. Each of the Hancock Building's four sides has the shape of a trapezoid (sort of a triangle with the top cut off). Therefore, all of the apartments inside the building have one wall that is at an angle. According to LaVey's logic, people living there might do crazy things—such as jumping out of high windows—because their apartments make them *feel* crazy.

Interestingly, since ancient times, trapezoids themselves have been thought of as "gateways" for paranormal forces. Perhaps the Hancock Building is a kind of gateway through which strange or even evil forces enter Chicago.

Whatever the reason, the strangeness of Streeterville certainly doesn't keep people away. Each year, millions of people come from all over the world to visit the historic and beautiful "Magnificent Mile." Next time you're shopping or sightseeing in the area, stop for a minute and close your eyes. Maybe you too will sense something sinister.

Holy Cow! It's Scary Harry.

5

A Ghost at the Ballpark: Scary Harry and the Curse of the Cubs

Wrigley Field—home of Chicago's usually awful National League baseball team—hasn't been haunted for too long. It's been only a handful of years since the death of Harry Caray in 1998. Harry was the long-time Cubs' announcer. He was famous for singing badly, wearing funny glasses, and shouting, "Holy Cow!"

Three Possible Ghosts

Harry is now believed to be Wrigley's resident phantom. Why do fans think Harry stayed behind? The reason, they say, is obvious. After Harry died, the Cubs began playing too well! Normally, the Cubs just weren't good enough to compete. Then, a strange and unexpected winning streak began. People started to believe that maybe some supernatural influence was at work.

In the fall of 1998, ghosthunters began investigating the possibility that Harry's ghost was indeed contributing to the Cubs' good luck. They discovered unusual electromagnetic energy in the bleachers. These seats are straight across from the announcer's box where Harry sat for years. Still, no strange activity was found in the box itself. Therefore, some believe that it's not Harry hanging around at all. Rather, it could be an unknown "Bleacher Bum"—one of the Cubs' famous fans—who may have died around the same time that Harry did.

Even before talk of a haunting by Harry, some fans believed that a musician named Steve Goodman was haunting the ballpark. In life, Goodman was a huge Cubs' fan. In fact, he wrote a number of songs about his favorite team, including *Go, Cubs, Go.* The singer loved the Cubs so much that he asked to be buried inside Wrigley Field under home plate. To everyone's surprise, the Cubs granted Goodman his wish. His ashes are there today!

The Curse of the Billy Goat

Whether or not Wrigley Field is actually haunted remains uncertain. No one is quite sure who or what might be hanging around this popular spot. What most Chicagoans do agree on, however, is that the Cubs themselves are *cursed*.

The curse was reportedly placed on the team long ago. One afternoon, a local tavern owner named William Siannis tried to take a goat inside Wrigley Field during a Cubs game. Siannis was trying to get publicity for his bar, the Billy Goat Tavern. When the gatekeepers refused to let the goat inside, Siannis put a curse on the team. The curse has supposedly kept the Cubs out of the World Series since 1945!

Since then, several people—including William himself—have tried to undo the curse. Almost every season, however, the Cubs keep losing a "paranormal" number of games. But what's even scarier? The team's fans still think that the Cubs are the greatest team around!

6

Bad-Guy Ghosts:
Scary ... Dead or Alive

Chicago is famous for its beautiful lake-front, stunning skyscrapers, and world-class museums, and attractions. The city is even more famous, though, for its criminals!

A lot of Chicago's well-known lawbreakers have been politicians, but most of the city's famous crooks have been robbers and gangsters. Many of them survived shootouts. Others avoided traps laid by po-

A Phantom Bad Guy at the Biograph

lice officers and FBI agents. Eventually, like everyone else, they met their deaths. Many of those criminals, however, refuse to pass on to a better place. Maybe they can't get in!

This might explain why Chicago has some of ghostlore's most unlawful spirits. Many of them like to haunt the city's Lincoln Park neighborhood. In the 1920s and 1930s, several gangsters lived in fancy apartment buildings in that area. Police officers or rival gang members killed some of these gangsters in their homes or as they left their buildings. Others were gunned down while carrying out crimes away from home. One of the world's most famous criminals was killed at the movies!

The Ghost of John Dillinger

In 1934, John Dillinger was Public Enemy Number One—the most-wanted criminal in America. That summer, many people had seen him hanging around Chicago's North Side. By the age of twenty, Dillinger had begun his life of crime by holding up his hometown grocery store in Indiana. He spent eight and a half years in jail before being let out early for good behavior. As soon as he got out, though, he robbed three banks in three months! He was caught again and went back to prison. His old prison mates soon helped him escape. In the next year, with the help of his gang, Dillinger pulled off six major bank robberies. He also killed two police officers, two FBI agents, and one civilian. In addition, Dillinger escaped from jail twice and avoided or shot his way out of at least six police traps!

John Dillinger was about to meet his match, though. A man named Melvin Purvis was head of the FBI in Chicago at the time. All he cared about was getting John Dillinger—dead or alive. Purvis had been trying to capture or kill the gangster for four months, ever since Dillinger had arrived in Chicago. North Siders had also been searching for Dillinger. They were terrified by reports that he'd been seen in their neighborhood.

Finally, on one hot July night, Dillinger walked into a trap. It had been set by Purvis outside the Biograph Theater on Lincoln Avenue. Dillinger had gone to the Biograph to see a movie with two women. They were his girlfriend, Polly Hamilton, and a lady named Anna Sage. When the movie was over and they came outside, sixteen police officers and FBI agents were waiting for them. When Dillinger saw what was happening, he took off. He ran down a narrow alley just south of the theater's front doors. A hail of gunfire soon stopped him, and he fell dead.

Some people believe you can still see John Dillinger's ghost running down that tiny passageway away from the police. Witnesses claim to have seen the bluish figure of a man who stumbles and falls . . . then disappears! Others who take the shortcut through the alley report that the passage feels cold even on the hottest summer days. This is a sure sign that a ghost is near.

St. Valentine's Day Massacre Ghosts

Not far from the Biograph Theater is the site of another famous "gangland" haunting: 2122 North Clark Street. This was the site of an old garage where a terrible shooting took place . . . on Valentine's Day!

In 1929, the two worst gangs in Chicago were run by George "Bugs" Moran and Al Capone. This was during the time of Prohibition when it was illegal to sell alcoholic beverages in the United States. Gangs throughout the country made lots of money producing and selling illegal alcohol. The gangs often got into fights with one another over this "business." In Chicago, the Moran and Capone gangs were always trying to become the most powerful one. Each gang tried to control more of the illegal alcohol that was bought and sold in Chicago.

On the morning of Valentine's Day 1929, some members of Bugs Moran's gang were gathered inside an old garage on Clark Street. They were awaiting the arrival of a truckload of whiskey. Because the weather outside was bitterly cold, the men tried to keep warm by standing around a potbellied stove. While they were waiting for the truck to arrive, four of Al Capone's men came into the garage. Two were dressed as police officers, and two were wearing dark suits and overcoats. All four were carrying machine guns. Moran's men were ordered to line up against the back wall. Then Capone's men shot them dead. At the time of the shooting, Al Capone was vacationing in Florida. He denied having any part in the "St. Valentine's Day Massacre."

Today, people walking by the site often hear screams and machine gun fire. The site of the massacre is now a parking lot for a high-rise building. When dog owners walk their pets along the fence there, the animals sometimes howl wildly at the lot or back away in fear! No one can deny that the ghosts of the murdered Moran men still hang out at the place where they died.

Al Capone's Ghost

As for Al Capone, he died in 1947. He was believed to haunt the old Lexington Hotel on 22nd Street, where he had his offices. After the hotel was closed, people looking through the windows sometimes saw a dark figure moving from room to room in the abandoned building. Then, after the Lexington was torn down, Capone's ghost reportedly moved somewhere else entirely. Now, his ghost is on board his old *yacht*. Some believe that since Capone can't get into Heaven, the yacht is the most peaceful place he can find!

7

Calvary Cemetery:
A Damp Spirit on the North Shore

Imagine driving one night along a dangerous stretch of winding road. On one side is a rocky shoreline with waves crashing against the stony embankment. On the other side is a spooky old cemetery, its tombstones awash in moonlight. Now, imagine that the headlights of your car pick up a figure in the road—a figure of a man. The man is soaking wet and covered with seaweed. He drags himself across your path

The Aviator

from the rocky shore toward the cemetery entrance. You swerve in time to miss hitting him. Then, you glance in the rearview mirror in time to see the figure reach up toward the cemetery gate and . . . disappear!

The Aviator

Well, *thousands* of drivers didn't have to imagine this scene. It actually happened to them along the dark and winding portion of Sheridan Road at the Chicago–Evanston border. This roadway runs between Lake Michigan and Calvary Cemetery. There, for more than twenty years, a drenched and dripping phantom made nearly nightly appearances. Sometimes, drivers maneuvering the tricky curve would spot a man dressed in flying gear and trailing strands of seaweed. He would haul himself up and over the stone embankment of the lake. Other drivers would nearly run him over as he dragged himself across Sheridan Road toward the cemetery gate. Still others would nearly drive off the road after seeing the figure disappear through the locked gate.

This phantom is called "The Aviator." Old-timers believe that he is the spirit of a World War II fighter pilot who drowned just offshore during training exercises over Lake Michigan. Some people even claim to remember just such a crash—and that the body of the downed pilot was never found.

The Sightings End

Whoever he may have been, the soaking wet spirit of Calvary Cemetery is said to have ended his escapades one night in the mid-1960s. Many believe that, on that night, the Sheridan Road gate of the cemetery was accidentally left open. This allowed "The Aviator" a chance to find a less watery grave inside!

Why would a ghost need to enter a cemetery through an unlocked gate? No one knows for sure. It seems certain that, whatever ended his escapades, the once high-flying phantom of Calvary Cemetery is enjoying a more restful afterlife. It only took him more than two decades of very active haunting.

Today, that little stretch of Sheridan Road is a lot less dangerous for drivers who venture along the North Shore at night. Still, for the many who remember their encounters with "The Aviator," the ride around that bend is still a scary and hair-raising trip.

A Shifting Totem Pole

8

The Lincoln Park Totem Pole: Sneaky Feats of a Mysterious Monument

The colorful and imposing totem pole in Lincoln Park seems a little out of place. You might expect to find a monument like this deep in the woods or in some other "natural" setting. In the shadow of towering high-rises along Lake Shore Drive at Addison Street, however, the pole just looks odd.

It may not be all that surprising, then,

that the totem pole itself seems to feel a little bit uncomfortable. In fact, some people say that one of its figures actually *shifts position*, as if it feels unsettled!

One of the totem pole's figures is a man holding a spear and riding a whale. For years, people have claimed to see certain changes in this figure. Some days, the man's arms and legs are in one position. On other days, the limbs will have shifted to a different pose.

Unbelievable? Some think so. Many people have seen actual photographs of these "changes." They claim that they are hoaxes or optical illusions. Many others, however, are very willing to believe that they're real. The believers just might be right. Native Americans themselves have long believed that totem poles have the power to come to life!

So, the next time you visit this mysterious landmark, take a closer look. Try and remember exactly where everything is. Then, make plans to come back another day. When you return, you may be surprised at what you see!

Rosehill Cemetery's Lulu

9

Rosehill:
A Gaggle of Ghosts

If you like haunted graveyards, you'll love Chicago's Rosehill Cemetery. It's got more than a dozen ghosts.

Rosehill is located along old railroad tracks on the city's North Side. When the cemetery was first built, the surrounding area was rural. Visitors—and bodies—had to travel by train from Chicago to this far-away burial ground. In fact, you can still see the old casket elevator. It was used to bring coffins down from the train tracks to the cemetery grounds below.

Ghosts of Little Girls

Ghosthunters don't have to look farther than the cemetery's front gate to see their first phantom. This is the spirit of a little girl named Philomena Boyington. She can sometimes be seen peering out a window under the funeral bell tower. Philomena was the granddaughter of William Boyington, the architect who built the cemetery gateway in the mid-1800s. She loved to go to work with her grandpa while his crew was busy building the entryway. Sadly, Philomena died of pneumonia not long after it was finished.

Another little girl also haunts Rosehill. Her name is Lulu Fellows. She is sometimes seen wandering around the graves near her own headstone and monument. A lifelike statue of her is encased in a glass box. Many visitors to the cemetery are very fond of Lulu. Often they leave gifts—coins, candies, and toys—at her gravesite.

Another tiny spirit is of a baby girl named Frances Pearce. It haunts the grave where Frances and her mother are buried. A beautiful glass-encased statue also marks this site. Some say that on their birthdays, the glass box fills with a fine mist. Then, both mother and daughter rise from the pedestal to greet any visitors that might be near!

Ghosts of Young Lovers

A high-school student named Elizabeth Archer is said to haunt the Archer–Fischel monument. After her boyfriend Arnold Fischel died in an accident, Elizabeth was so sad that she killed herself. Her ghost is sometimes seen visiting the monument on chilly November evenings.

The spirits of another young couple are reported to haunt the cemetery near the intersection of sections 11 and 18. They are thought to be the spirits of young lovers who died after taking a drug overdose. They killed themselves because their parents didn't want them to get married. Many visitors who have reported seeing the couple. A funeral director and a priest even say they have actually *talked* to the ghosts . . . and that the ghosts vanished soon afterward!

Eerie Sightings Connected to Evil

Also at Rosehill is the monument built by the Lincoln Park Masonic Lodge. This club was shut down after its members were accused of practicing black, or evil, magic. A huge ball weighing several tons sits atop the club's monument. According to rumors, the ball falls off its pedestal every ten years. Some say it's a sign from Heaven that the club's members are being punished for the bad things they did.

A shady character buried in Rosehill is Gerhardt Foreman. He was a friend of Alistair Crowley, who was once known as "the wickedest man in the world." Like his pal,

Foreman dabbled in black magic and other "devilish" pastimes. People say his tomb was chained shut to keep him inside!

Rumors of evildoing also surround the tomb of Darius Miller. He is believed by some to have died from the curse of King Tut, along with the rest of the team that unsealed Tut's tomb in 1922. Every year on May 1, Rosehill employees have seen a blue light seeping from Miller's tomb in the early morning hours.

Strange sights are also reported at the grave of Mary Shedden. She was supposedly poisoned by her husband. Many people have seen Mary's face appear on her grave-stone. Some have seen a lovely, smiling face. Others have been terrified by the vision of a leering skull.

Other Rosehill Ghosts

Much less frightening is the lifelike statue of a deer that marks the Frank M. Baker grave. An image of this sculpture is sometimes seen "grazing" near the cemetery gates, far from the Baker plot.

The noisiest ghost at Rosehill is the spirit of Charles Hopkinson. He is sometimes heard rattling chains in his mausoleum near the Ravenswood Avenue gate.

The most famous of the cemetery's phantoms is the ghost of Richard Sears. He was the founder of the Sears and Roebuck Company. Sears's mail-order catalogs and stores became very popular with shoppers back in the 1800s. Sears and his family are entombed in a quiet family room in Rosehill's community mausoleum. This is a huge concrete building filled with thousands of tombs. Sears's family seems to rest peacefully enough, but Richard himself is restless. His ghost—dressed in fancy black clothes and a top-hat—is sometimes seen walking through the mausoleum. At other times he is seen staring from the door near his family's tomb.

Finally, even Rosehill's old caretaker is

said to get into the ghostly act. After being murdered in his home nearby, he continued reporting for work—and still does. Visitors and employees sometimes see him as he was in life. His ghost is dressed in overalls and leans on a shovel near the retaining vaults behind the cemetery's May Chapel.

Hawrar Takes a Nighttime Stroll

10

The Field Museum: Naturally Scary

Have you ever been scared on a school field trip? If you've ever spent the day at Chicago's Field Museum, the answer must surely be yes! This natural history museum has more than twenty million specimens in its collection. It's not surprising that at least a few specimens send shivers down the spines of its visitors. Two exhibits in particular have long been called haunted. Weird sights and sounds occur in the halls where they're housed.

Ghosts of Egypt

One of these haunted exhibits is called "Inside Ancient Egypt." It includes displays of many priceless Egyptian artifacts—including mummies. Visitors to the exhibit love to examine the mummies' ancient *sarcophagi* (coffins) and learn how the mummies' bodies were preserved. Some people, including museum employees, think that one of the museum's mummies is not quite dead, even after thousands of years!

The mummy's name is Hawrar. He is reported to escape from his sarcophagus at times to take nighttime walks through the museum. Security guards know when he's on the loose because they occasionally hear his sarcophagus crash to the floor. When the guards investigate, they almost always find Hawrar's coffin several feet from its display stand.

No one has actually *seen* a mummy wandering around the halls of the museum at night. Some of the museum's employees, however, have reported seeing shadowy "visitors" long after visiting hours have ended. Those who have seen them are convinced that these visitors are not quite real. They apparently have a tendency to vanish into thin air!

Growling Ghosts

Another of the Field's eerie exhibits is the display of the famous "Man-eaters of Tsavo," a pair of enormous stuffed lions. When they were alive, the lions became famous for a horrifying reason. They *ate* almost 140 bridge builders in Africa.

Such lions are not normally dangerous to humans. An outbreak of disease, however, had killed off many of the animals that the lions would hunt for food. The lions were then forced to eat whatever else was available. That included people working on the bridges.

The lions terrorized the people of their region over a nine-month period in 1898. Lieutenant Colonel John Henry Patterson finally shot and killed them. He sold the lions to the Field Museum in the 1920s. Ever since the lions were placed in the museum, visitors say the big cats sometimes growl, move, or disappear altogether!

11

Woodlawn Cemetery: The Circus That Never Leaves Town

Pet owners have long told stories about being visited by the ghosts of their beloved animal companions. After death, these pets stick around to haunt their masters. Many former pet owners have felt the sensation of fur nuzzling against their legs or of tiny paws creeping across their sheets as they lie in bed! Non-human ghosts such as these

The Circus at Woodlawn Cemetery

are said to haunt one Chicagoland cemetery. These are not the spirits of dogs and cats, though, but of elephants!

For almost ninety years, visitors to Woodlawn Cemetery in Forest Park have reported hearing the distinctive sound of the trumpeting animals. They also occasionally have heard the roar of lions and tigers. These sounds are heard while walking through the graveyard's unusual section of plots called "Showmen's Rest." This area was set aside many years ago for the burial of circus performers. Visitors can easily find the section because it is marked by unusual but beautiful stone elephants.

A Deadly Train Crash

Some people believe that the ghostly animal sounds are from the spirits of those killed in a tragic circus train wreck. The crash occurred near Ivanhoe, Illinois, in 1918. On the day of the crash, about four hundred circus performers and employees were riding the Hagenbeck–Wallace Circus Train. It was headed for Hammond, Indiana. The horrible accident took place because another train was traveling on the same track. Both trains plowed full speed into each other. A number of the cars were wrecked. The crash resulted in a huge explosion and a deadly fire.

Eighty-six passengers died in the crash. Most were never identified because a great number of the circus performers were known only by their nicknames. Even today, many of the graves at Woodlawn Cemetery are marked only by names such as "Baldy" or simply as "Unknown Male."

Where the Sounds Came From

Legend has it that some of the circus animals on the train died trying to rescue their trainers. Some of the animals burned to death as they dragged away pieces of fiery wreckage. Some people believe that it is the ghosts of these dead animal-heroes who wail at Woodlawn. They are lonely over the loss of their circus friends.

Of course, people who don't believe in the paranormal have their own explanations for these strange animal sounds. They say that on windy days the breeze carries to the cemetery the sounds of the elephants and lions living in nearby Brookfield Zoo! It's eerie, they admit, but not exactly supernatural.

Nevertheless, whether you believe or not, a visit to Woodlawn Cemetery—with its sad gravestones and huge stone elephants—is indeed a haunting experience. Take a trip there some windy afternoon and see—or, rather, hear—for yourself.

Father Damen, in Touch with the Paranormal

12

Holy Family Church: The Paranormal Life— and Afterlife—of the Famous Father Damen

Along Roosevelt Road, on the city's Near South Side, stands one of the oldest houses of worship in Chicago: Holy Family Roman Catholic Church. Next door to the church is Saint Ignatius College Preparatory High School. Outside the school's front entrance stands the statue of a serious-looking man dressed in a long robe. This is Father Arnold Damen. He was the priest at Holy Family who founded St. Ignatius. According to legend, he has never left.

Every Chicago ghost lover knows that since his death the priest has haunted both the church and the school. Many, however, do not realize that during his lifetime Father Damen himself had many brushes with the paranormal. These experiences began during the Great Chicago Fire.

The Great Fire broke out in the fall of 1871. At that time, Chicago was a young but quickly growing city. On October 8, along with the rest of the city, parishioners at Holy Family Church were terrified. They had learned that a huge fire had broken out during the night. It was growing bigger and bigger by the hour. As the fire spread, the anxious parishioners realized that the flames were moving right towards their neighborhood. The fire was threatening to destroy not only their homes but their beautiful, almost brand-new church as well!

The Power of Prayer

Father Damen was an energetic and enthusiastic priest. He also had very strong faith. When he learned that the church was in danger, he sent word to his parishioners to drop everything they were doing. He told them to pray hard that their church would be saved.

"Pray that the fire will somehow miss us," Father Damen told them. "Pray that the fire will go around the church."

His advice seemed pointless. The giant wall of flame was headed directly for Holy Family. The fire was so big that it had already burned everything in its path, and it was still getting bigger! Nevertheless, the parishioners at Holy Family prayed . . . and prayed . . . and prayed.

Then a miracle happened. Just as the fire had nearly reached the church, the wind shifted. The flames began shooting in another direction, away from Holy Family. The parishioners were stunned. The church was spared. Father Damen wasn't surprised at all, though.

In thanksgiving, the people of Holy Family placed a statue of the Virgin Mary in the front of the church. Mary is sometimes called "Our Lady of Perpetual Help," and this is what the parishioners called her. They believed that she asked her son, Jesus, to save their church from certain destruction.

A Vision in the Night

Father Damen seemed to be in touch with the supernatural world at other times, too. One night, a number of years later, he was sleeping in the rectory where the church's priests lived. He suddenly saw two boys standing at the foot of his bed. Father Damen sat straight up. He recognized them right away. They were two brothers who belonged to Holy Family Church. Father Damen knew the two because they served as altar boys, helping the priests during Mass. The boys were dressed in their cassocks, or church robes. They looked as if they were ready to serve at Mass right then, in the middle of the night. They were even holding lighted candles, just as they would at church services.

The boys didn't say a word, but Father Damen sensed they wanted him to follow them somewhere. He got up and dressed. Then, he followed them outside into the street. The boys led Father Damen through the neighborhood, to a run-down little house a few blocks away from the church. Once there, the three passed into the house and down a long hall to one of the bedrooms. Inside, Father Damen found an old woman lying in her bed. She was obviously very sick and dying.

Father Damen knelt down at the woman's bedside and began to pray. He said the prayers that make up the Last Rites of the Catholic Church. They prepared the woman for her death. Then, he stood up and left the woman and the boys. He returned to his room at the rectory, where he returned to bed, and fell fast asleep.

In the morning, Father Damen didn't remember anything that had happened during the night. He had forgotten all about the strange visit from the boys, the silent journey to the run-down house, and the old woman with whom he had prayed. As he sat eating his breakfast, the housekeeper told Father Damen that one of the parishioners, an old woman, had died during the night.

"You knew her well," the housekeeper told him. "She was the mother of those two brothers—the altar servers who drowned last year."

Father Damen was stunned. Suddenly, he remembered everything that had occurred the night before—especially the faces of the boys he had seen. Though he had recognized them right away, he hadn't realized that they had been dead for many months! The boys had appeared to him and had taken him to their dying mother. They wanted to make sure that she received the church's Last Rites.

None of the parishioners who heard this story were surprised. Ever since Father Damen's plea for prayers had saved the church from the Great Fire, he was thought to have some sort of special connection to the supernatural. The parishioners thought that midnight meetings with ghostly visitors seemed normal for Father Damen!

Father Damen's Own Ghost

Of course, it also seemed normal when, after his own death in 1890, Father Damen was seen by parishioners in Holy Family Church. Fellow priests also saw him in the rectory where he had lived. Most often, though, the students at St. Ignatius High School saw him. Because Father Damen had founded the school, he loved the place and the students more than anything. After his death, he continued to stroll the school's halls. He kept an eye on the students and made sure that everything was running smoothly.

Even today, students at St. Ignatius still see Father Damen. Sightings especially happen whenever the century-old building is being repaired in some way. During the 1980s, a number of students reported seeing the old priest walking through the hallways. No doubt he was examining the work that was being done inside the school at the time. One student even saw him open the door of a locked room and walk inside. When the staff unlocked the door, they discovered that *the entire floor of the room had been removed* as part of the building's repairs. There was nowhere the priest could have gone!

13

Bachelors Grove Cemetery: Mischief Makers and Magic Houses

Imagine walking down a deserted path through the woods and seeing a quaint, old house in a nearby clearing. You feel strangely drawn to the place and start walking towards it. The closer you get, though, the smaller the house becomes until . . . POP! It disappears completely!

This is only one of the many bizarre things people have seen at Bachelors Grove Cemetery. This wooded cemetery is south-

Bachelors Grove Mysteries

west of Chicago. It is one of the most haunted places in the entire world.

In the 1830s, German settlers first made their homes in these woods. "Batchelder Grove" was probably a family name given to their burial ground. Another story tells that a group of single men first settled there, leading to the nickname of "Bachelors Grove."

Strange Sightings

Wherever the name comes from, Bachelors Grove has been a favorite spot for ghosthunters since the 1950s, when the road leading to it was closed, cutting the graveyard off from traffic. Since that time, the area has been isolated. Visitors have had to park across the road and go on foot down a long, wooded dirt path to the graveyard. Along the way, some people have seen the shrinking "Magic House." Strange lights also appear and chase visitors through the woods. Mysterious cars sometimes show up out of nowhere and nearly run folks off the road. Then, the cars vanish into thin air!

Over the years, Bachelors Grove's eerie stories have drawn many curious people to the cemetery. Sadly, some of these visitors have been vicious vandals. They have gone so far as to dig up graves and move tombstones. Some believe that these vandals have angered the spirits of the people buried there. This has made the cemetery even more haunted than it may have been in the first place.

Explanations for the Hauntings

No one is really sure why this little graveyard should be the site of so many strange goings-on. Some stories say that after Chicago gangsters killed their rivals, they would drive the bodies to the cemetery. Then the gangsters would dump the bodies in an adjoining pond. A legend says that the "phantom cars" seen racing nearby are the ghost cars of these murderers.

Another story says that, many years ago, the cemetery's old caretaker went crazy and killed his family. Afterwards, he burned their house to the ground. According to believers, this is the "Magic House" that is sometimes seen by people walking in the woods.

However, there are many other weird happenings at Bachelors Grove that seem to have no "explanation" at all. One involves the ghost of a woman in white carrying a baby in her arms. Also seen from time to time are figures dressed in black robes. Strange faces also appear on the cemetery's old tombstones.

A psychic once visited the cemetery. This psychic believes that *all* of the people buried at Bachelors Grove must remain there as ghosts for a period of time. Then, they can finally rest in peace. This would certainly explain why such a tiny place should be so haunted. If the psychic is right, it means that some two hundred spirits are haunting an area only one acre in size!

Francis Leavy's Handprint

14

A Ghost in the Firehouse: The Hand of Francis Leavy

Many ghost stories describe places that have become haunted after tragic fires. Have you ever heard of a haunted *firehouse* though? Chicago firefighters have long told just such a story. It is about the firehouse that once stood at 13th Street and Oakley Avenue on the city's West Side. It was the home of Engine 107 and Hook and Ladder 12.

A Prediction Comes True

The tale begins on the morning of April 18, 1924. That happened to be Good Friday, the Friday before Easter. A firefighter named Francis Leavy, known as Frank to his buddies, was going about his morning chores at the firehouse. Another firefighter named Ed noticed that Frank, who was usually very cheerful, seemed to be sad about something. Ed asked Frank if anything was wrong, or if he was upset about having to work that coming Easter Sunday. Frank had been washing the windows of a firehouse door. As he paused to answer, he rested the palm of his hand on one of the soapy windows. Frank replied that nothing was wrong. As Ed turned to go, though, Frank said something else: *"This is my last day with the fire department."*

Ed was startled that Frank would say such a thing. Before he could ask Frank what he meant, the alarm bell started ringing through the firehouse. The firefighters ran to put on their helmets, coats, and boots. They then climbed aboard the engine and ladder truck.

The men figured they were going to help fight a big fire at the Union Stock Yards, which had been burning for many hours. They weren't. Instead, they had been called to a fire at an office building called Curran Hall, just south of downtown. The trucks sped to the fire, dodging cars, horses, and streetcars. Ed tried to talk to Frank above the noise. Ed was frightened by what Frank had said back at the firehouse. He was anxious to find out what his friend had meant.

Before Ed could get his answer, the men arrived at the fire. The building was well ablaze. A number of firefighters were ordered to go up to the second floor and put out the fire burning there. They went inside and struggled to control the fire, but something terrible happened. The outside wall of the building began to crumble.

Fire chiefs standing outside in the street began screaming to the firefighters inside to come out quickly. The warning came too late. Before they could get out, the falling walls crushed most of the men inside the building. Frank Leavy was one of the unlucky ones. Legend says that hours later when eight dead firefighters were pulled out of the ashes, Frank Leavy was the only one who could be identified.

The Handprint on the Glass

The next day was a grim one for the men of Engine 107 and Hook and Ladder 12. They had lost a number of their fellow firefighters in the fire at Curran Hall. They spent most of the day sitting around talking about what had gone wrong. While they were talking, Ed suddenly gasped and pointed to the window of the firehouse door. There on the glass was the image of a man's hand! That was exactly where Frank Leavy had rested his palm when he'd spoken his mysterious words.

Spooked by the handprint, Ed rushed to

get a bucket of soapy water and a towel to wash it away. *It wouldn't come off!* Each of the firefighters there took a turn trying to scrub off the eerie print. It wouldn't budge.

For days afterward, the firefighters attempted to get the handprint off the window. They used all kinds of soap. When that failed, they tried getting it off with ammonia, but had no luck. They even tried to scrape it off with a razor blade. Finally, they called the glass company that made the window. Someone from the company came to remove the handprint. Even their strong chemicals didn't work.

Pretty soon, Frank Leavy's handprint became famous. Newspaper reporters, firefighters from other firehouses, and curiosity-seekers of all kinds made the trip to the little firehouse. They all wanted to see the strange handprint on the window. One day, a city official brought a copy of Frank's fingerprints from city files. He compared them with the handprint on the window. *Indeed, they matched perfectly!*

Finally, the firefighters stopped trying to remove the handprint. For twenty years it remained on the window, as clear as the day Frank had made it. Then, on April 18, 1944, a newspaper boy accidentally threw the morning paper through the window. The glass shattered to pieces. This happened exactly twenty years to the day of Frank's death.

Even though the glass had been broken, nothing could shatter the legend of Frank Leavy's window. Long ago, the firehouse at 13th and Oakley was torn down. Today, however, the story of Frank's handprint is still told by old firefighters to new recruits. Although no evidence remains to prove that the handprint had ever existed, Frank Leavy and his mysterious mark live on . . . in the stories and hearts of firefighters all over Chicago.

15

Graceland Cemetery: An Endless Game of Hide and Seek with the City's Littlest Ghost

If you have a really good arm, you might be able to hit a baseball out of Chicago's Wrigley Field and into Lake Willowmere. This is the small pond in nearby Graceland Cemetery. If you went hunting for your home run ball, you could also take in some great ghosthunting at this legendary graveyard. Many well-known Chicagoans are buried here alongside many not-so-famous

Inez Clarke, One Resident Ghost of Graceland Cemetery

citizens. Regardless of their fame, they all seem to "co-exist" in happy harmony.

Some Graceland Legends

Most of Graceland's paranormal legends are no more than just good ghost stories. For example, no one has actually *seen* the green-eyed "ghost dog." This dog supposedly guards the entrance to the underground tomb of Ludwig Wolff. Still, people who live in the apartment buildings just beyond the cemetery's fence say that the dog howls all night long whenever the moon is full.

Nor has anyone ever looked into the eyes of Lorado Taft's famous sculpture *Eternal Silence* and, according to folklore, caught a glimpse of their own death. The sculpture is nicknamed the "Statue of Death" and is located next to the tomb of Dexter Graves. It is probably the most popular monument in the entire cemetery. The dark, hooded figure of *Eternal Silence* has scared plenty of visitors who have come to see it.

The Death of Inez Clarke

Of Graceland's many ghost stories, one stands out as being more believable than the rest. That is the story of a little girl named Inez Clarke. Some historians claim that Inez never existed. Still, many people report having seen her ghost near the beautiful statue that bears her name.

According to the story, Inez died of tuberculosis when she was only seven years old. In the late 1800s, it was not uncommon for deaths to occur at a young age. Advanced medical knowledge and medicines were not available to treat serious diseases.

Inez was an only child, and her death left her parents full of sadness. In her honor, her parents, who were very rich, had a lovely sculpture made for her grave. It looked just like Inez, with long, curly hair and a pretty smile, wearing her favorite dress and holding an umbrella. The statue was so beautiful—and so lifelike—that strangers came to Graceland just to see it.

The Disappearing Statue

Sometimes when visitors showed up at Inez's grave, they would find that the statue was missing. Disappointed, their next stop would be at the cemetery office. There, they would ask whether the statue was being cleaned or repaired. They would also ask when it would be returned to the gravesite so they could come back and see it. In reply, the confused cemetery workers would insist that the statue was right where it should be. After walking the visitors back to Inez's grave, however, the workers would be shocked to find that the heavy sculpture was, indeed, gone! What's more, every time these "thefts" were reported to police, gravediggers would find the statue back in place, with no sign of damage.

Soon, the cemetery workers got fed up with the incidents. They decided to do something to stop the mischievous people who, they thought, must be stealing the statue as a prank. A solid glass case was built to protect Inez's sculpture and to prevent its removal. The glass case was fastened securely to the base of the statue so that it could never be stolen again. Nevertheless, after a few nights, a security guard making his rounds came upon Inez's grave. Sure enough, the glass case was still in place, but the statue of Inez was gone!

Today, the beautiful sculpture of Inez Clarke still stands at Graceland—at least most of the time. The glass case remains there, too, protecting it from "thieves." As always, it doesn't seem to do much good. Many visitors to Graceland still find that the statue has disappeared.

Where Does the Statue of Inez Go?

A few stories have tried to explain the disappearances. One says that because the statue is so lifelike, it has confused Inez's spirit. The spirit believes that the *statue* is Inez's body. When the spirit enters the statue, it is able to run and play just as Inez did during her brief lifetime. This, the story insists, became so much fun for Inez that to this day she continues to run around the cemetery. She doesn't realize that she's dead!

Another, story is more sinister. This one says that Inez's sculpture only disappears during big thunderstorms. It then reappears after the storms have passed. Those who believe this story are convinced that Inez did not die from tuberculosis. Instead, she died when a bolt of lightning struck her during a storm. According to this story, Inez's parents carelessly left her locked outside during a terrible rainstorm. When they realized what they had done, it was too late. Because Inez's death came so suddenly, the little girl never realized that she was dead. When her wandering spirit saw the statue over her grave, it happily moved into it. Now, during loud, scary thunderstorms, little Inez becomes terrified. She runs away and hides until the storm passes and the sun comes out again.

Whichever story you believe—if you believe any of it at all—the grave of Inez Clarke is worth visiting. As you stroll through beautiful Graceland, you just might come upon a joyful little girl dressed in old-fashioned clothes. Don't be surprised if she is delighted to find a new playmate!

16

Horace Greeley Elementary School: No Floating in the Halls!

Can you imagine what it would be like if your school were haunted? The students who attend Chicago's Horace Greeley Elementary School don't have to wonder. None other than the ghost of Horace Greeley himself haunts their school. What's more, they claim that Greeley's ghost even *followed* them from the old school building when the new school was built!

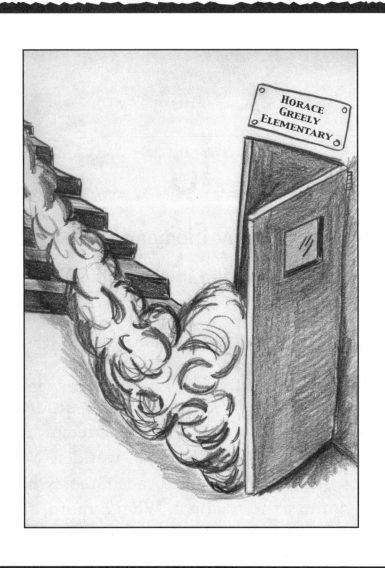

Horace Greeley's School Spirit

An Eerie Teacher

Talk of the "Greeley Spirit" began at the old building during the early 1970s. That was when a new and strange woman began teaching at the school. Many kids believed that the new green-eyed teacher was a witch. Other teachers noticed that she seemed to possess an eerie, almost mesmerizing control over her students.

One day, two teachers and a student were talking in the hallway outside the library. The strange woman teacher and her class entered the hallway and walked into the library. Then something happened! An enormous "cloud" that looked like a huge ball of fog rolled out of the library. The student and two teachers watched in horror as the cloud, floating several feet off the floor, passed by them. The cloud then snaked its way *up* the stairs and *around* the corner into the strange teacher's classroom!

Of course, none of the other teachers believed the story. Even the strange teacher herself denied having anything to do with the bizarre incident. However, the student who had seen the cloud told her friends that she had seen a ghost. Then, the tale spread quickly through the school.

The Ghost of Horace Greeley

Somehow, a rumor began that said the ghost was that of the school's namesake, Horace Greeley. In the 1800s, Greeley was a famous newspaper publisher in New York. The students were convinced that Greeley's spirit haunted his portrait that hung in the school library. For many years, students and teachers alike reported creepy happenings, especially in the library. There, among other things, students saw books plop off the shelves.

No one knows for sure whether the ghost of Horace Greeley really haunted the old Greeley School. Students at the "new" Greeley school (now more than twenty years old) are sure, however, that the old phantom followed them to the current school. Strange things still occur. Students and teachers alike remain convinced that their school's namesake is close by. If Horace Greeley himself is an honorary, invisible student, there is sure to be plenty of school "spirit" to go around!

The Bride and the Baby

17

Mount Carmel: The Bride and the Baby

One of the eeriest gravesites in all of Chicagoland lies inside Mount Carmel Cemetery. This cemetery is in Hillside, Illinois, a suburb just west of Chicago. No, this grave is not that of Al Capone, the most famous of Chicago's gangsters, although he is buried there. Rather, this grave is the eternal resting spot of a supposed saint. A spot that will definitely send a chill down your spine!

A Young Woman Dies

In 1921, Julia Buccola, a young Italian-American, died while giving birth to her baby. This in itself was very sad. Even sadder was the fact that the baby died, too. Julia's father was heartbroken over the loss of his beloved daughter. Julia was placed in her coffin dressed in her wedding gown and veil. The baby was laid in her arms. They were buried together at Mount Carmel.

Not long after the funeral, Julia's mother began having nightmares about her dead daughter. In them, she saw Julia calling to her, begging to be dug up! As these nightmares went on for six years, Julia's mother became more and more terrified. Finally, she decided to have Julia's body unearthed.

When the day arrived, Julia's mother went to the grave with a group of grave diggers. The workers dug up the ground. As they pried open the lid of the coffin, Julia's mother held her breath. She expected to see something ghastly. To her surprise, despite the passing of six years, Julia's body was still perfectly preserved. Not a hair was out of place, and her skin had stayed smooth and flush. What's more, Julia's white dress remained spotless, just as on her wedding day.

An Unsolved Mystery

At first, Julia's mother thought that some strange coincidence must have preserved the coffin's contents. Maybe the tight seal of the coffin had kept air and dampness from damaging Julia's skin and clothing. But why not those of the baby? The baby had been buried in Julia's arms. Unlike Julia, the baby's body and clothes were completely decomposed.

Julia's mother never understood why her daughter had haunted her dreams and asked to be dug up. The question of why Julia's body had been so well preserved remained a mystery too. Julia's family and friends were convinced that it was a miracle.

They believed that her preserved body was a sign from God recognizing Julia's warm and selfless spirit. From this, they concluded that she was a saint. The preservation of her body was undoubtedly proof that since she had been so good, she would be granted everlasting life.

Since her reburial, many people have come to agree that Julia Buccola is, indeed, a saint. However, the Catholic Church has not recognized her as one. Nevertheless, around Chicago, Italian-American women preparing for childbirth pray that Julia will help them deliver a healthy baby. Julia's story is very well known among other ethnic groups, too.

Visitors are drawn to Mount Carmel from all over. They come to see the "Italian Bride" statue on top of Julia's headstone. They also see the eerie black-and-white photograph attached to the front of the marble monument. The picture shows Julia lying peacefully and comfortably in her coffin on the day that she was dug up!

18

Navy Pier
Come Dancing . . . with the Dead!

Both Chicagoans and out-of-town tourists love Navy Pier. Each year, millions of them visit the pier. They enjoy its theaters, restaurants, arcades, shops, giant Ferris wheel, gardens, and old-fashioned lemonade and ice cream stands. Many people attend dinners and conventions in the grand ballroom at the end of the pier. Tour boats also line the pier to take people for short trips on Lake Michigan.

The Navy Pier Ballroom

A Deserted Navy Pier

Not that long ago though, Navy Pier was as deserted as a ghost town in the Old West. There were no shops, no music, and no lights. Only a few fishermen spent their days angling along the pier's concrete banks.

The pier's buildings themselves were mostly abandoned, including its former grand ballroom. The ballroom had once been one of the nicest, fanciest dance halls in Chicago. During World War II, the ballroom was shut down. The U.S. Navy used it as a school to train airplane mechanics. After the war, the University of Illinois at Chicago used the ballroom as a gymnasium. When the school moved to its new campus a few miles away, the heat was turned off in the buildings on Navy Pier. Chicago's brutal weather began to eat away at the ballroom's beauty. The copper ceiling started to leak, and pieces of the roof began falling in. Before long, weeds were growing between the cracks of the beautiful old dance floor. Security guards made matters worse. They used the walls for target practice!

A Ghost in the Ballroom

One hot August night, a lone security guard set out on a routine walk to the far end of the pier. Upon reaching the tip of the pier, the guard stopped to gaze out at Lake Michigan. The night air was still, with little breeze. A few boats filled with people bobbed up and down on the water. The beacon on the nearby lighthouse shone from the harbor. After relaxing for a few minutes, the guard began his long walk back to the security office at the front of the pier.

By that time, it was after two o'clock in the morning. The guard decided to walk through the buildings. He checked to make sure that everything was locked and secure. When he entered the old ballroom, his eyes took a few seconds to adjust to the darkness. He walked across the old wooden dance floor. Suddenly, he *felt* someone coming up from behind, although he hadn't heard a sound. Terrified, he reached for his gun and whirled around. *No one was there.*

No sooner had the guard turned around than a freezing cold chill passed through his body! As strange as it seemed, the guard was sure that a man, or rather the *ghost* of a man, had passed right through him. As scared as he'd been, the guard told no one what he'd felt inside the old dance hall.

A year later, the guard returned to the ballroom with a friend. This friend had psychic abilities. She could sense things that other people couldn't. The guard thought that his friend might be able to communicate with the spirit he'd felt on that hot August night.

Sure enough, the psychic sensed a ghostly presence right away! She felt that the spirit of a man who had often gone dancing with his wife haunted the ballroom. The man was waiting for his wife to die so that she could be with him. Then, they

could dance together in the ballroom for-
ever!

Today, no one knows whether or not Navy
Pier's ballroom is still haunted. These days,
it's as beautiful as ever and often full of life.
It's too noisy and too crowded for people to
notice any ghosts that might still be hanging
around.

Still, the next time you're at Navy Pier,
take a walk to the far end. Peek into the
windows of the grand ballroom. Imagine
that you see people dressed up in fancy
clothes, dancing the night away. Close your
eyes and try to hear the music of the big
bands. Then, close them a little tighter.
Perhaps you will feel someone else there—a
man who loved to dance . . . and, maybe at
long last, the lady he was waiting for.

19

Montrose Point: Strange Stories from the "Magic Hedge"

Chicago birdwatchers love to visit the peaceful lakefront area known as the "Magic Hedge." This is a winding path that is home to rare and beautiful birds. Another name for this area is Montrose Point. There, Montrose Avenue meets Lake Michigan.

After World War II, Montrose Point was far from peaceful. In fact, it was an army base and missile site! American soldiers

Pique and the Magic Hedge

were stationed at Montrose Point. They guarded the United States against attacks from its enemies, especially the Soviet Union. Hundreds of men were assigned there. Not all of them got along.

Two Fighting Soldiers

One pair of soldiers in particular never seemed to stop fighting. Their names were Pique Nerjee and Hernando Rodrickkez. Pique and Hernando were always arguing. They argued about who would clean the barracks' bathroom, whose turn it was to keep the midnight watch, whether that day's lunch had been any good, and so on. Sometimes their arguments became so heated that they ended up in a fist fight. The other soldiers soon got sick of breaking up their brawls.

One Halloween night, Pique and Hernando were going at it as usual over some silly thing. After their argument came to blows, the men in the barracks pulled them apart. Then Hernando started yelling, "I'm going to kill you, Pique!"

Pique swallowed hard and stared at Hernando. Though their fights had often been bad, neither man had ever made such a threat. Luckily, Hernando had a Halloween party to attend. He simply shook his fist at Pique and stormed out of the barracks. Pique breathed a sigh of relief.

One Dead Soldier

Later that night, when the soldiers were all asleep, they were suddenly awakened. They heard a strange noise that they couldn't quite place. When they got up to look around, they found Pique dead in his bed!

No one could imagine what might have happened. When the coroner arrived, even he was baffled by Pique's death. The young soldier had always seemed perfectly healthy. More doctors arrived to examine

Pique's body. Suddenly, someone ran into the barracks screaming Pique's name. It was Hernando!

Hernando's eyes were as big as dinner plates. He had obviously been terrified by something he'd seen. When he saw Pique's lifeless body on the bunk, he began sobbing hysterically. He pleaded, *"Pique! Pique! Please, Pique!"*

Pique's body was finally taken away. The other men calmed Hernando down, which took a long time. When Hernando was finally quiet, they asked him what had happened on the way back to Montrose Point.

Hernando explained that he'd been at the Halloween ball. Everything was fine until, during the middle of a dance, he suddenly felt that something had happened to Pique. He rushed out of the ballroom and back to the barracks. When he saw that Pique was dead, Hernando was convinced that it was his fault. Hernando thought that he'd somehow wished Pique dead because of their argument earlier that evening.

When the men heard this story, they tried to convince Hernando that he wasn't to blame. Hernando only got worked up again. He insisted that Pique's blood was on his hands. Then, without warning, Hernando jumped off the bunk. He ran out of the barracks into the cold November night. *He was never seen again.*

One Missing Soldier

All night, the soldiers at Montrose Point searched the area for Hernando, but with no luck. Another search during the day also led to nothing. Several weeks passed with no sign of Hernando. Finally, he was declared dead. The army assumed that Hernando had jumped into the freezing waters of Lake Michigan and had drowned.

The next year on Halloween night, soldiers on patrol at Montrose Point saw strange figures moving in the Magic Hedge. Then they heard a low, moaning sound, like a voice saying, *"Pique! Pique! Please, Pique!"*

The soldiers searched the whole area with their rifles ready, but no one was there.

By the next Halloween night, the army base at Montrose Point had been closed down. All the soldiers were gone. Two homeless men, however, were sleeping in the park at Montrose Point. They told police that "vampire bats" had attacked them during the night. The bats had whispered that they wanted to suck their blood! The police assumed that the vampire bats were probably just some rare birds or owls and that the men had dreamed they'd heard voices.

Nothing more was reported at Montrose Point until a few years ago. One Halloween night, sanitation workers were doing some emergency sewer work. They saw a strange light running through the Magic Hedge. When they investigated, they found no one in the area. The workers did report a low, moaning voice, however. It sounded as if it were saying, *"Pique! Pique! Please, Pique!"*

Ghostly Glossary

bizarre: Strange; weird.

casket: A coffin.

eerie: Describes something that gives you the creeps!

electromagnetic: A kind of energy that ghosthunters study using special devices called *EMF meters*. Changes in a place's *electromagnetism* can tell a ghosthunter that a ghost may be near.

mesmerizing: Describes something that has a hypnotic or spellbinding effect.

parapsychologist: A scientist who studies the paranormal.

paranormal: Anything unexplained by normal science. Ghosts, poltergeists, life-after-death experiences, and even UFOs and other baffling things are all said to be paranormal.

phantom: A ghost.

presence: Something that you can't see but

can definitely feel—like an invisible ghost.

psychic: A person who claims to be able to see or communicate with ghosts (a *medium*), read other people's minds (*telepathic*), be aware of far away events or objects (a *clairvoyant*), or of events before they happen (*precognitive*).

retaining vaults: Storage places at a cemetery where bodies were kept during the winter. Before machinery was invented for digging through the hard, winter ground, the bodies of people who died during the winter months had to be stored until the spring thaw, when the ground could be dug up by gravediggers.

supernatural: Describes a thing or event that is not a part of the natural world as scientists understand it. Ghosts and other paranormal things and events are said to be supernatural.

sacred: Describes a place or object thought to be holy or to have religious or spiritual energy.

sinister: Dvil, unlucky, or just plain bad.

A Ghosthunter's Tools

These days, even beginning ghosthunters often use lots of high-tech tools in looking for ghosts. All sorts of expensive gadgets can be used, from *electromagnetic field (EMF) meters* that detect paranormal energy changes, to *night-vision goggles* for seeing in the dark, to *thermal scanning guns* that help find the "cold spots" associated with ghosts. But you don't really need a lot of technology or money to search for spirits. With a bag of simple and cheap tools, you can match wits with any ghosthunter. Just remember that the two most important tools can't be bought or battery-operated: these are *patience* and *luck*!

A **flashlight** is very important, as you will want to do your investigating in as much darkness as possible. Ghosts love the dark!

A **watch** is useful for telling the time at which strange events occur. You can also do regular journal "entries"—either in a note-book or by talking into a tape recorder—at specific times (say, every fifteen minutes).

A **camera** may help you catch a ghost on film if your timing is right. Some ghost-hunters take photos around "cold spots"—the patches of cold air that are caused by a ghost absorbing all the heat. If you have an instamatic or Polaroid camera, you may want to use it instead of a regular one. These cameras seem to be better at captur-ing ghostly images.

A **tape recorder** is good for interviewing witnesses and also, as mentioned above, for recording a "journal" of your investigation. Simply record entries every fifteen minutes or so, telling the time and any activity that you or your team members have experi-enced since the last entry. You can also do "sweeps" of a haunted site with the tape recorder on, going from room to room or area to area and stating where you are. Later, if ghostly voices or other sounds show up on tape, you can do more investigating in that room or area.

A **compass** can detect strange changes in the magnetism of an area, possibly telling you when a ghost is near.

Fishing line or thread and **tape** can help you figure out whether objects, such as furniture, are really moving. Tape one end to a wall and one to the object. If the thread breaks off, you may want to do some more investigating. Fishing line is also good for finding out if living people are playing tricks and causing the "paranormal" activity. Tape a piece of line across the doorway to each room. Then, if something weird happens in a room and the line across that door is broken, you'll know that a human—not a ghost—caused it.

Baby powder can also be used to trap human trick-players. Powder sprinkled on the floor of "haunted rooms" will easily show the footprints of someone who has been fiddling around in a haunted area, causing objects to move, making noises, or opening and closing doors.

Salt or sugar can be sprinkled around small objects that seem to be moving around. If the object moves, it will make a little path in the salt or sugar. Also, if you're nearby, you'll hear the "crunch"!

A **measuring tape** can help you figure out whether an object has moved, how much a door has opened or closed, or how far a ghost seemed to travel before disappearing!

A **notebook and pen** can be used to write down all sorts of information, from interview questions and answers to a log of paranormal events and the times at which they happened.

Interview Questions for Witnesses

If you're interested in getting started as a "real" ghosthunter, the most important thing to remember is that ghosts are *elusive*—that means that they are never around when you want them. No matter how much fancy ghosthunting equipment you have, you're probably not going to find too many ghosts who are willing to be photographed, recorded, or otherwise "caught" by a ghosthunter. So, in order to learn about a haunted site, you will probably have to rely quite a bit on information you get from interviewing witnesses—people who have already experienced the paranormal phenomena or events at the place you're studying.

It helps to have some good questions in mind when you ask people about their experiences. This keeps you on track and also helps to put the people you are interviewing at ease. They will see that you're a professional who is taking them and your job seriously. The following list may be helpful to get you started:

1. *What is your name and age?*

2. *Do you believe in ghosts?*

3. *Do you believe in the supernatural?*

4. *What have you experienced at the site? Describe sights, sounds, and smells, as well as "feelings."*

5. *When did the experience take place?*

6. *What time of day was it?*

7. *Did you have the experience more than once?*

8. *Was anyone else with you at the time? If so, did they have the same experience?*

9. *Do you know if anyone else has experienced the same thing or similar events at this site?*

10. *Do you know of anything in the site's history that might explain the paranormal* *events, for example, a murder or death?*

11. *Were you aware that the site was "haunted" before you had your own experience there?*

10. *What do you think caused the event you experienced? A ghost? A hallucination? Something else?*

11. *Have you had other paranormal experiences besides the ones at this site?*

12. *Is it okay if I use your name when speaking to others about your experience?*

Recommended Reading

For readers interested in learning more about ghosthunting, there are a number of great books available to help you learn the basics of phantom-finding.

Auerbach, Loyd. *ESP, Hauntings and Poltergeists: A Parapsychologist's Handbook*. Warner, 1986.

Taylor, Troy. *The Ghost Hunter's Guidebook*. Whitechapel Productions, 2001.

Guiley, Rosemary Ellen. *The Encyclopedia of Ghosts and Spirits*. Facts on File, 2000.

Cohen, Daniel. *Young Ghosts*. Dutton, 1994.

Deem, James. *How to Find a Ghost*. Avon, 1988.

De La Rosa, Shelia. *Ghost Files*. Disney, 1997.

Spencer, John and Tony Wells. *Ghost Watching*. Virgin, 1994.

Usborne Reader's Library. *Tales of Real Haunting*. EDC Publications, 1997.

Usborne. *Usborne Book of Ghosts & Hauntings*. Usborne, 1999.

Those interested in learning more about Chicago's ghostlore have these resources:

Bielski, Ursula. *Chicago Haunts: Ghostlore of the Windy City*. Lake Claremont Press, 1998.

Bielski, Ursula. *More Chicago Haunts: Scenes from Myth and Memory*. Lake Claremont Press, 2000.

Clearfield, Dylan. *Chicagoland Ghosts*. Thunder Bay Press, 1998.

Crowe, Richard T. *Chicago Street Guide to the Supernatural*. Carolanda Press, 2000.

Kaczmarek, Dale. *Windy City Ghosts*. Whitechapel Productions, 2000.

Seekers of state-wide spirits will want to check out:

Taylor, Troy. *Haunted Illinois*. Whitechapel Productions, 1999.
This is only one of Taylor's many books of ghost stories, all of which you can learn about at www.historyandhauntings.com.

Index

Ursula Bielski

Ursula Bielski grew up in a haunted house on the North Side of Chicago and still lives in that same neighborhood with her own family. At an early age she became a believer in paranormal experiences, from the curse of the Chicago Cubs at nearby Wrigley Field to the ghosts at local Graceland Cemetery. In college Bielski tagged along with psychology students investigating reported hauntings, and she has been a ghosthunter ever since.

Her interest in the apparent relationship between folklore and ghostly activity led Bielski to write the acclaimed and widely successful book, *Chicago Haunts: Ghostlore of the Windy City*. A second volume, *More Chicago Haunts: Scenes from Myth and Memory*, was released in 2000. She also co-authored *Graveyards of Chicago: The People, History, Art, and Lore of Cook County Cemeteries*. This is her first book for younger readers.

Order Books by Ursula Bielski

Creepy Chicago   _____ @ $ 8.00 =_____
Chicago Haunts   _____ @ $15.00 =_____
More Chicago Haunts   _____ @ $15.00 =_____
Graveyards of Chicago   _____ @ $15.00 =_____

Subtotal: _____
Less Discount: _____
New Subtotal: _____
9% Sales Tax for Illinois Residents: _____
Shipping: _____
TOTAL: _____

Name_____

Address_____

City_____**State**_____**Zip**_____

Visit our Web site at <u>www.lakeclaremont.com</u> to learn about our other books on Chicago and Chicago history.

Please enclose check, money order, or credit card information.

Visa/Mastercard#_____**Exp.** _____

Signature_____

Discounts when you order multiple copies!
2 books—10% off total, 3–4 books—20% off,
5–9 books—25% off, 10+ books—40% off

—Low shipping fees—
$3.00 for the first book and $.50 for each additional book,
with a maximum charge of $8.00.

Order by mail, phone, fax, or e-mail.
All of our books have a no-hassle, 100% money back guarantee.

P.O. Box 25291
Chicago, IL 60625
773/583-7800
773/583-7877 (fax)
lcp@lakeclaremont.com
www.lakeclaremont.com